Destination

Serenity

Journey into Serenity

Daily Interactive
Journal and Affirmations

Daquian H. Williams

GrindTime Publishing Group, INC.
Columbus, OHIO

Grind Time Publishing Group, Inc.
5440 Lonsdale Place South, Suite D.
Columbus, Ohio 43232

Ordering Information:
Quantity sales. Special discounts are available on
quantity purchases by corporations, associations,
and others. For details, contact the
"Special Sales Department" at the address above.

Destination Serenity/ Daquian H. Williams. -- 2nd ed.
ISBN 978-0-9831611-5-8
Library of Congress Control Number: 2022936229

This book is dedicated to my daughter Serenity, along with my loving Mother Sikeena, Grandparents, Family, and Friends

Love the ones that have always been there for you at your lowest and your highest. Spend time, and share laughter and knowledge with the ones who you didn't have to call because they already know you. Care for the ones that care for you.

"Serenity is the tranquil balance of heart and mind."

-Harold W. Becker

CONTENTS

Will YOU Accept the Challenge?

Much like Destination Serenity Volume 1, we will hit the ground running, taking full control of the magical life YOU were blessed with. Your mind is the most prestigious muscle, tool, and wonder in the world we live in.

In the blink of an eye, you literally can create the next cure, win an Oscar, build the next model of housing or car, and design the next set of technology to hit the markets.

You are a true game-changer and we cannot sleep on any of that. We will change the way we think, and act to that will elevate us beyond the level of happiness, success, knowledge, and life we vision to reach.

Before we get started on your journey to serenity; we first have to recite the following:

"The paths I take in my life are much different fromthat of the next person.

Life will give me opportunities through disaster, pain, struggle, and high and low points to find who I am and my passions.

Every day we will begin prepping our minds to start our individual journeys to conquer and reconstruct our minds to achieve greatness and find peace with who we are."

You are now ready to accept the challenge to bring positive thoughts, words, knowledge, and actions to my everyday life.

<u>Challenge Starts Now!</u>

We Are Challenging You to Become a Better "You" Every Single Day!!

Adults you are Queens and Kings

Children, you are Princesses and Princes growing to be Kings and Queens.

Words are everything, always remember we are Royalty and we address each other as such it creates a sense of empowerment for the other person that naturally builds up who we are as an individual.

A gesture this small to yourself and those around us every day can start to boost confidence, and allow us to begin making those moves you thought were only best fit for someone else; forgetting you are Royalty and there is nothing that is not suited for you.

To Better Days

Start every day, by taking your daily dosage of motivation; in the mirror, repeat aloud those affirmations to yourself, your partner, kids, family, friends, roommate, whomever you choose to share your positivity with every day!

Always **BELIEVE** what you are saying

Speak **POSITIVELY** into your life

Words are **POWERFUL**

And can become your daily **ACTIONS**

Yesterday Is **HISTORY**

Welcome to Stage Two of Destination Serenity

Normally, you will be challenged mentally and physically.

It is okay not to have all the answers, we are not God.

There will be times you break down or lash out, you are not at a standstill or the end of the road. You are merely learning how to deal with your triggers or specific situations in life. Now learning how not to react poorly or in a way you will regret is your assignment when the challenging time may come. Conquering your mind and creating your mental capacity will come in very uncomfortable measures.

You will test yourself.

Train your mind.

Begin to challenge your actions and reactions

Expose any doubts as you will become comfortable with being uncomfortable and creating a will when there is a way is key.

Failure will seize, now looking at any failures as a mere lesson that will create a blessing for you.

Constant repetition creates the structure needed to always be on top of YOU.

None of these traits will come easily, but by constant repetition, you read those affirmations in the mirror and challenge yourself daily to develop and expand your mind.

Persistence and constant Grind will become your everyday proteins building who you are.

Will you have to accept the challenge to challenge your mind and actions on the road to Serenity?

Challenge of the Day

List three ways to communicate or interact with an individual or group to express yourself in a noncontroversial manner.

1..
2..
3..

Challenge

Definition

A task or situation that tests someone's abilities.

Repeat Out loud

I was born to define odds and embrace challenges with a full mind and body. I cannot look at challenges of any sort as a hindrance in my growth but as a clear-cut advantage to strengthen the growth process and gratification when the challenges have been overcome.

Motivation

Positively communicate your feelings the entire day. Knowing communication is one of the most important functions we will do daily and the key to much of life's beauties, and curses; rather than be nonverbal, physical, mental, spiritual, or verbal communication. 98% of communication is done by listening, another 1% of communication comes from our bodies and the last percentage is us actually speaking.

You never have to overwork communicating.

Starting a conversation and gaining someone's respect can be as simple as you saying "How's your day going today?"

Even when communicating with someone is not in your best interests you can still diffuse that communication gap by addressing the person properly, directly, and respectfully; allowing the other party to know that you do not want to communicate with them.

Today's Challenge

What challenges do you face throughout your life?

Do you battle with overcoming those challenges?

Create a list below of 10 small healthy challenges to better yourself that you will accomplish within 21 days from now because you can!

Narrow Minded

Definition

Not willing to listen to or tolerate other people's views; not willing to accept opinions, beliefs, behaviors, etc. that are unusual or different from one's own. A state of deliberate personal limitation.

Repeat Out Loud

Open my mind, free my soul, experience life's treasures, nothing has ever been impossible

Motivation

There will be many family members and close friends who are living life with a closed limited mindset, and such trait reflects in their professional careers, entrepreneurship goals, and traveling opinions.

This is fine, however, once these people begin to bring your vision to match or fit into their vision you are no longer giving your vision the love and care that they need.

Listening to such closeness can begin to give you feelings of discouragement, and doubt. Living life on the approval of others will lead you to a life of stagnation and limitation.

Opening your minds does the trick, but closing out your dreams will default to emotions that you find hard to cope with and "What if," "Shoulda," "Would of could of," statements.

Today's Challenge

List 15 challenges around the world that people are fighting daily?

What are your feelings towards other individuals' struggles?

What techniques best help you overcome adversities?

DAY NINTY-THREE

Hatred

Definition

Intense dislike or ill will.

Repeat Out loud

I will not allow hatred to consume my life. Holding on to grudges is never healthy. Not forgiving allows anger to boil over time, it is a state of self-imprisonment that restricts the functioning of the soul. Anyone who hates my faithful doings will become a piece of my daily motivation.

Motivation

Growing up far too often I would hear my grade school teacher and principal telling me I would not make it to my high school graduation. Family members also told me I will be in jail before I turned sixteen years old. Your so-called friends talking bad about you. In a city where many tell you they are hoping death wasn't our only option before we were able to prove anyone wrong, tough skin was worn like armor.

Negative energy becomes a form of hatred when continuously spread. Words are so powerful they will dagger through the mind like the wild thorn of bushes. Actions of hate will pierce through the body like a bullet

The objective is to move on with our life without attachment to where our feelings of hate arise or the feelings of hate others show us. Hate is a learned tribute

Today's Challenge

Why do you feel hate?

How can you resolve these feelings?

Have you ever felt that someone has shown emotions of hate towards you?

How did that hate make you feel?

Definition

The quality of being honest and having strong moral principles; moral uprightness.

Repeat Out loud

No matter what room I walk into or what doors are closed, I will always remain myself. Respecting myself and others around me no matter where I am or how others are acting. I am wise enough to admit my wrongs and brave enough to know when being true to myself or those around me is being taken advantage of. Hi

Motivation

The greatness of a man or woman is not in how much wealth, material, or the popularity he acquires, but as the late Bob Marley states "greatness comes from their integrity and ability to affect those around them positively."

The strength of a nation derives from the integrity of the home.

– Confucius

Today's Challenge

What does the word "integrity" mean to you?

List the qualities one may possess that qualify the person to be lacking good integrity?

Honor

Definition

Adherence to what is right or to a conventional standard of conduct.

Repeat Out loud

Every morning I wake is a blessing, I will remain true to myself, and those around me.

Motivation

Honor yourself, your core values, and those who have honored you. Honoring anyone or anything blindly can become our worst enemy. It could become detrimental to our honor. When we keep a clear mindset and faith, we begin to feel peace throughout our lives.

It is not our purpose to become each other; it is to recognize each other, to learn to see the other, and honor him for what he is.

- Herman Hesse

Today's Challenge

What do you honor?

What are the Pros and Cons of what you Honor?

Can you honor something that possesses negative energy or intentions for yourself? If so, how do you combat such?

Definition

Honesty implies a refusal to lie, steal, or deceive in any way.

Repeat Out loud

I will always be honest with myself; I do not need to lie to anyone about anything present in my life.

Motivation

Being honest doesn't take effect until you've realized the facts of not being honest; the detrimental effect of dishonesty on oneself. It clogs our progress in life.

Please read the above sentence again. Far too often we don't realize the damage of not telling the truth until the damage has been brought to the light.

We are not perfect, let me be the first to tell you about the young me. I was the king of the little white lie thinking that being completely honest isn't the easier task, that sometimes hanging unto that little white lie could solve a lot of problems within itself.

I realized the older I got and after a few arguments, fights, and suspensions just how much damage one white lie can cause and there is not one person on earth worth lying to. Lying puts you in deeper situations where you have to continue to lie.

"Honesty is the first chapter in the book of wisdom"
                    Thomas Jefferson

Today's Challenge

Do I feel good after not being honest?

Why lie to cover the true feelings of myself or someone else?

Do I deserve to be lied to?

How can a little blue become a big disaster?

Definition

Reflecting politeness in one's attitude and behavior toward others.

Repeat Out loud

Having good thoughts for others is my first step preceded by positive actions that create true happiness. When I wake up, I will no longer think of just me but think of the entire world. Every person, object, species, animal on this earth as I want to be treated.

Motivation

Free your spirit, become one with all around you. Feed your soul, love, and hope, help your neighbor, honor thy stranger as you honor your faith and hope.

"And let us not be weary in doing well: for in due season we shall reap, if we faint not."

Galatians 6:9 (KJV)

Today's Challenge

Compliment 20 people this week with no expectation of them returning the gesture

Write how doing good for others makes you feel?

Politeness

Definition

Behavior that is respectful and considerate of other people.

Repeat Out loud

Every time I think of a scenario of being rude, I revert to thinking what if I or one of my loved ones were treated in such a manner!

Motivation

I was always told to treat the janitor as if they were the CEO of any business. We all are blessed and granted life accordingly. Disrespecting or belittling others only hurts ourselves in the long run.

A lot of times, we truly never know who we are being rude to, or even if we do, we may never know the mental damage we could be causing to others.

A few years back, sometime in 2016, I was just turned twenty-two years old. That faithful day, I was outside playing with my niblings. I noticed an older gentleman crying as he walked by our yard.

Being concerned, I couldn't let him walk by without asking. After stopping him I asked, "Sir are you okay?"

He responded you will see my face on the news tonight.

Confused and unsure of what he meant, I asked him what was going on? That I was there to listen without judgment or response unless he wanted me to give him one.

The gentleman told me this would be the last day he speaks to anyone, and I'm the last person who will hear his voice. He told me he was going to the bridge less than a mile away to jump over in an attempt to kill himself.

Instantly, I stopped everything I was doing and planned to attend to the man I just met. My niblings watched me hugging this fifty-eight-year-old man who was in tears and asking what is wrong.

After several minutes of just aiding a brother back to a place of peace without too many words but mainly by just listening.

I asked him what makes him happy and told me the things he has accomplished and others he is yet to accomplish. I asked why he was feeling this way.

He told me he was a retired veteran and loved teaching martial arts, and the reason he wanted to take his life was that his children stopped reaching out to him, he lost his job, and felt as if he had nothing or anyone to live with for. The pain I felt from this King's heart could make 1000 Lions kneel in surrender.

I then told the kids this man here wants to show you what makes him happy and we will show him why his test is special no matter what he's going through and that testimony will bless the lives of many people to come.

We sat, talked, and played with the kids for the next hour. Before you know it, we exchanged contacts, he had a new destination far away from the bridge. A mindset that still to this day, we talk and are eager to learn, teach, and love those who were once in his shoes facing that same walk to the bridge.

Based on confidentiality, I will not list any names but this story will always resonate with me. One small gesture can change the life of many. You never know what someone is going through.

Today's Challenge

List ten examples you have seen where handling a situation politely has benefited someone?

List ten examples or how many you can think of that you witnessed when not being polite or thoughtful of others went wrong?

How can you become more polite?

What is the opposite of polite?

Which category would you rather be considering?

Definition

The practice of being or tendency to be optimistic in attitude.

Repeat Out loud

I will speak positively into my life every single moment of my life. I know words will lead to actions and actions will lead to Better Days. Speaking positively to others is just as important as speaking positively to me, when good is done or said repetitively to others good faith and blessings follow.

Motivation

The power of positive speaking can amount to endless opportunities and added happiness in your life.

Growing up, I had a lot of negative reinforcement from outside my circle, and even deep inside my circle, friends, family, and those around me daily. To some people, it was just that moment of being in our life. I had many people telling me I wasn't anything, literally in their own words. I've been called many names, and even returned the favor with negative thoughts and words as well as being involved in acts of violence because I allowed negative situations and energies to overwhelm who I am and what I stand for.

The one thing I noticed as a young adult, athlete, parent, friend, family member, and one that genuinely cares for the happiness of others was the power of thoughts and words.

We can move mountains and elevate above all negatives when we inject positivity into our minds and words daily.

My God and ancestors both endured pains, words, and actions done to them that we can only imagine but every single moment they had the chance to speak positive or do positive through all the adversities, chains, blood, separation, tears, anger, and negativity surrounding them.

We are a piece of both of those groups, and no one can take that away from us, and with that, we will continuously grow.

Today's Challenge

Name a time when you allowed negativity to overpower your actions or words?

Research five people or groups that literally were treated horrible but overcame with positivity?

Remember that positivity is practiced every day

Volunteer and Give back

Practice talking positively to yourself daily

Listen more to everyone

Learn more from those who are where you want to reach

Forgive yourself and others.

DAY HUNDRED

Definition

Consideration for the needs of other people and careful thought process

Repeat Out loud

When I think of those who genuinely care about me I will always win. I'm not perfect but my actions show every day I am worth it.

Motivation

Be thoughtful with every action. Considering the thoughtfulness and generosity youextended same to you will create healthy family knit bonds, even if they are not blood relatives, and better enhance your physical and mental state.

Today's Challenge

Ask someone you care for what their passions and dreams are?

Where can you be of help while chasing your passions and dreams?

Why is being thoughtful in your daily actions important?

Persistent

Definition

Continuing firmly in a course of action despite the difficulty or opposition..

Repeat Out loud

I will constantly push toward my visions and remain persistent in making sure I am who I want to be with every breath I take.

Motivation

We all were born to achieve greatness and reach peaks never seen before, however, the majority of us do not remain consistent with keeping faith in our dreams.

Far too often it becomes easy to stop or those butterfly feelings of the unknown leading you to thoughts of wanting to quit. We must overtake those negative feelings preventing us from reaching our ultimate goal.

After reading this sentence, close your eyes and place yourselves inside a plane!

Now the pilot just announced that they did not want to complete the flight, they rather take a break proceeding to leave the cockpit.

What would your thought be if you were on this plane!!?

No matter how hard the road can get when you set a vision you drive through that tunnel knowing light is at the other end.

You got this!

Today's Challenge

What can you do to help eliminate stress or anger in situations that don't meet your outcome?

What activities make you happy?

Surround yourself with positive people

Assertive

Definition

Having or showing a confident and direct personality, dialogue, or action

Repeat Out Loud

I will become of service to my faith and reposition my life to how I want my life to be. I will move assertively knowing my dreams and passions will not be accomplished unless I work relentlessly. I will not allow any negative words, actions, energy, or even those thoughtless excuses we can all create to justify our reasons for not moving forward with achieving our ultimate vision of who we were meant to be.

Motivation

No more excuses as to why you cannot become happier and more fulfilled with the wonderful life with which you are blessed.

Assert yourself to the best scenarios possible to achieve your dreams.

Logic will get you from A to B Imagination will take you everywhere.

~Albert Einstein

Today's Challenge

No more excuses towards why you cannot achieve greatness

What is your definition of greatness?

What are the steps you will take to achieve your greatness?

Creativity

Definition

The tendency to generate or recognize ideas, alternatives, or possibilities that may be useful in solving problems, communicating with others, and entertaining ourselves and others.

Repeat Out loud

My mind ignites the strongest fuel this earth possesses. I can change my tomorrow today. I will not be afraid to reach outside of the box and create my own box

Motivation

A Queen once told me the place with the highest ruined talents and unused ideas was the cemetery or graveyard and it instantly hit me.

As humans, we are blessed to have the ability to be creative every single moment of our lives

"You can't use up creativity the more you use the more you have."

-Maya Angelou

Today's Challenge

Take 30 mins today to write any and everything you wish to

Create a list of goals attached with how you will accomplish them

Create something new today no matter what it is.

Innovative

Definition

Innovation, as a concept, refers to the process that an individual or organization undertakes to conceptualize brand new products, processes, and ideas, or to approach existing products, processes, and ideas in new ways.

Repeat Out loud

I will act on those thoughts and innovate new changes in the world. I am a world changer, different from many. I will disrupt the normal process of thinking and create paths never trodden before

Motivation

The only way to discover the limits of the possible is to go beyond them into the impossible

Arthur C. Clarke

If we never become comfortable with being uncomfortable, we will always be in a place of comfort which can never allow us to grow from that place

I used to be terrified of failing due to being naturally competitive and accustomed to winning. I would not do specific challenges just because I wasn't sure what the outcome would be.

The first day I stepped outside of those comforts I fell in love with being uncomfortable and learned that failing is a beautiful gameplan to how to do it right the next time

Today's Challenge

Think New! List ten things not yet created or put to action in the world

List changes you want to see made in the world we live in

List your initial steps into making these changes come to action

Definition

Not a copy or imitation; present or existing from the beginning; first or earliest

Repeat Out loud

Who I am is who I'll be. Unique in many of my ways. I will always remain original to who I truly am.

Motivation

When we mention just how special you are and why being yourself is so important, you must remember that there is not another you.

Even biological twins are not completely the same.

There will never be another you!

One of the easiest tasks for ourselves is to be who we truly are. There are no standards of anyone or anything you need to act, dress, or talk like at all.

You have no one to impress

Your family, friends, kids, and those in the world will love you for you.

Stay Original and True to yourself always

Today's Challenge

Have you ever felt as if you had to compromise who you are to fit into a specific group?

What made you feel as if you did have to compromise yourself? If not explain why you did not compromise yourself?

List ten phrases or actions to help you never feel as if you need to be someone you are not?

Studious

Definition

Spending a lot of time studying, learning, researching done deliberately or with a purpose in mind.

Repeat Out loud

My mind is worth everything, becoming more aware and studious about the world around me, I will learn to love the act of obtaining more knowledge.

Motivation

Learning to love learning is not an easy task. Many of us have to acquire such traits and work even harder to maintain those advantages given to us. However, once we capture within our minds that our brains are our strongest organ/ muscle our light bulbs will begin to flash in our minds. When our minds are exercised correctly, greatness will rise from our depths of struggle, and trial and error.

Research, actually doing, and obtaining knowledge becomes essential to everyday growth.

At a very young age, I found the more I enjoy learning, I can align myself for greater success in life.

This came after countless nights of what I thought as a young child were dreadful punishments of reading dictionaries, researching different careers of influential people creating the greatest pleasure of knowing I too am Greatness

Today's Challenge

Never be too scared to put yourself into a predicament to learn and grow personally whether the results are good or bad. The act of actually doing, and engaging in the practice, regardless of whether you are prepared captures more neurons within the mind than that from a phone or computer. Far too often everywhere you go many have allowed phones and computers to become our peace and saviors and our only source of learning. You learn more from doing.

Today, challenge yourself to experience something new.

What did you learn from your new experience?

Definition

To furnish knowledge and give someone greater knowledge and understanding about a subject or situation.

Repeat Out loud

The mind is powerful, I know teaching others not only benefits my learning process but allows me to share my knowledge to grow the minds of others on getting their desired paths.

I will enlighten all who seek my knowledge and I cross paths knowing our thoughts can become our realities.

Motivation

O Holy Spirit, descend plentifully into my heart. Enlighten the dark corners of this neglected dwelling and scatter their cheerful beams.

Saint Augustine

Today's Challenge

For the next 21 Days challenge yourself to learn something new every day and share your knowledge with a different person daily

Become a student of the earth. Your answers will not be found from magic gurus you must focus, push yourself, and overcome to achieve.

Empower

Definition

Make someone stronger and more confident, especially in controlling their life and claiming their rights.

Repeat Out loud

Empowering my thoughts is key, empowering those around me is a gift, I am able, I can do it and I will make it happen

Motivation

Respect others' free will.

Honoring someone's choice is easy when we agree with somone. It's more difficult when we don't agree. That's when empowering them becomes so vital to show you still care and are there for them regardless of their decision.

When we constantly wish to better our lives and those around us, we can take control of our daily actions consecutively. Consistency in doing will not allow your full potential to rise to the levels you are seeking. Taking little action toward your goal continuously, day after day is better than never.

Daquian Williams

You have the recipe to inspire, uplift, and empower

Today's Challenge

Speak your affirmation to yourself in the mirror every single day confidently stating that you can do it, you are royalty, smart, and ready to change the world.

Definition

Give support, confidence, or hope to someone or something

Repeat Out loud

My life has never been a blemish, challenges became beautiful lessons in disguise, pains and sadness switch to instant gratification and happiness. I am more than phenomenal and encourage not only myself but those around me to be the greatest versions of themselves every day

Motivation

"Character cannot be developed in ease and quiet. Only through experience of trial and suffering can the soul be strengthened, ambition inspired, and success achieved."

Stephen King

Today's Challenge

How can encouragement alter the mind?

Do you encourage happiness in those around you? If not, what can you do to begin to encourage others to be happy with themselves?

Inspire

Definition

fill someone with the urge or ability to do or feel something.

Repeat Out loud

Every day, I will inspire myself to reach greater depths into my passions. I will begin to create a legacy of inspiration through mypassions.

Motivation

Story of the lost girl

A gentleman was walking through the woods when he spotted a crying girl, and he noticed that the girl had ropes on her hands and feet as if she was held captive in a cage.

The man asked the young girl why she was crying and why she had ropes on her arms and feet?

The girl responded, smiling from ear to ear as she looked across the Ohio River pointing at a house with a small picket fence on the other side of the river.

She mentioned that her whole life, she was held captive, she was being told every day she wouldn't amount to anything and was only allowed to leave her room to use the bathroom. Since she was a baby, she was told and she also believed that if she took these ropes off, she will be cursed for the rest of her life.

As the man gazed upon the house in the oasis, he was completely in shock and confused. Asking himself why the girl didn't try to leave the house to get help sooner.

All that was holding her back from escaping the house, was a small piece of rope tied to one of her legs and attached to her arm, and that little white picket fence.

Curious and wanting to know the answer, the gentleman asked the girl why didn't escape if you were in danger?

The girl replied;

"When I was very young and much smaller, they used the same size rope to tie down my brothers and me.

Every day, we were told there is nothing outside of this farm and if we left past that fence we will be killed or eaten to death by an animal in the woods. As we continue to grow up, we condition our mind and body to never test the unknown, this is our reality and escaping that cannot be accomplished.

We believed those words, threats, and physical restraint were enough to never go beyond the horizon for years but I believed that light across the river was freedom."

The only reason that the girl nor her family weren't breaking free from the house or the reality that was outlined in their mind. Over time they adopted the belief that it just wasn't possible to leave the home or life they were living.

No matter how much the world, someone, or any obstacles within your life try to hold you back, always continue with the belief that what you want to achieve is possible. Believing you can become successful, and that you can be at peace. Happiness is the most important step in actually achieving your success and peace within the life you live.

The little girl believed there was better beyond that fence of negativity, although she battled with weathering the storm for years, she never let that light of Better Days fade away, and nor will you.

Today's Challenge

What, Who, or even Where have you been inspired?

What traits of yours do you feel you need to sharpen?

Definition

The status, right, or power of an individual or group to be successful, famous, or highly regarded

Repeat Out loud

I am Royal

No one can take that from me

No person or action can tell me that I don't deserve to live every day I wake to my fullest potential

Motivation

"But ye are a chosen generation, a royal priesthood, a holy nation, a peculiar people; that ye should shew forth the praises of him who hath called you out of darkness into his marvellous light:"

1 Peter 2:9 KJV

You were chosen from birth to be Great

To Lead
To Smile
To Vision
Then Execute

You were chosen to be You

Nobody on this earth can be You

Today's Challenge

In what ways can you mentor and help others in your life regardless of circumstances or age?

List 20 reasons why you are Great?

*Remember there is nobody in the world exactly like you. Let's think about this question a little bit longer.

You are the real deal and there is not another like you.

Let's tap into why you are royalty.

Definition

Form a mental image or concept.

Repeat Out loud

The mind is limitless, we can imagine our most creative thoughts without any physical proof of actual creation. I have the power to orchestrate my wildest thoughts into physical actions, inventions, businesses, networks, and even relationships. I will begin to dream of my most innovative goals and strive to conquer each one.

Motivation

Close your eyes for 20 minutes taking deep breaths

Relax your body and mind

Now begin to imagine a window in front of you shining bright as amber-gold walls across the Pacific Ocean

Find your peaceful place and walk into that light

Walk through the light imagining your peace and happiness.

Once you have reached a mental zone of ultimate peace or discomfort open your eyes

What did you see?

Today's Challenge

If you can create anything in the world that has not been created, what would it be?

How will I plan the thoughts from my imagination into the world?

Definition

Form a mental picture or idea of an object, person, or thought.

Repeat Out loud

Imagine life with limitless boundaries. All I have to do is to dream and achieve.

Motivation

If my mind is the strongest weapon I posse on this earth, then my imagination has to be the ultimate ammunition to conquer the spectrum of reality unknown at this current moment

Today's Challenge

Take 30 minutes today, close your eyes and imagine accomplishing everything you vision.

How do you feel you can make your visions come to light?

Invest

Definition

Devote one's time, effort, or energy to a particular undertaking with the expectation of a worthwhile result.

Repeat Out loud

I will invest in my happiness, traveling the world, indulging in endless moments of happiness, and enhancing my mind to ultimate heights I will invest in myself.

Motivation

It wasn't until I was staring down the barrel of a 38 revolver that I realized your peace is all that matters. As the bullet came streaming out, the muzzle directly passed my ear atpoint-blank range, life, people, dreams, and smiles flashed into my mind at airplane-like speeds crashing through my mind.

Visions of my last day on earth pouring into my head, all of the goals set I have not yet accomplished and people I didn't say goodbye to.

I thanked the Most High after I realized I was untouched and remembering life has a way of reaching you, by showing exactly why you should value your mind, actions, body, soul, and spirit. Enjoy the moments in life that make you smile. Cherish those who love you for you. Become at peace with who you are and who you are becoming.

The life we live is precious

Today's Challenge

List goals you want to accomplish in your life and what the initial investment whether time, finances, or even hardships you will encounter before prospering in the fruits of your investments.

If you could be an investor, what would you invest in?

Definition

A feeling of great pleasure and happiness.

Repeat Out loud

Find joy in all of those around me, myself, my actions, and even in those struggles life twists into the spectrum filled with darkness there in the undertone lays joy

Motivation

Allowing others and situations to control your mind leads to cement blocks constantly being built around your emotions. Feeling as if you cannot be happy or enjoy your life is the absolute opposite of what we are learning through the lessons in our life.

It's been hard moments throughout life for all of us that we don't wish to speak about in the public. Death, Violence, Societal new norms, Uncontrolled Emotions, Feelings of loneliness and so many negative variables weighing on us but allowing those feelings to conquer the mind enables the outlets of the mind to think or the body to act in a negative light.

These negatives can have you moving differently, feeling as if you can't accomplish specific goals set in front of you and feeling caged, taking an unadvised risk of not being able to control emotions.

Today's Challenge

What makes you angry?

How can you turn those triggers into laughter or positivity?

How can you regain your peace once interrupted?

Excitement

Definition

A feeling of great enthusiasm and eagerness.

Repeat Out loud

I will be excited and cherish every little accomplishment for myself and those around me.

Motivation

Without leaps of imagination or dreaming, we lose the excitement of possibilities. Dreaming, after all, is a form of planning.

Gloria Steinem

Today's Challenge

Excitement can be disguised by fear, nerves, anxiety, and even sadness due to the direct correlation with feelings of overjoy.

What gets you excited positively?

What gets you excited negatively?

Definition

Arouse or inflame an emotion or situation.

Repeat Out loud

Ignite the flame, trust myself to achieve the unthinkable, become happy with all that I have, and Grind for all that will come to me.

Motivation

Your purpose every day you wake is driven by your passions, and your passions ignite your purpose.

"Take action once a day to do something that ignites your life."

Gabrielle Bernstein

"It only takes one match to ignite a haystack or one remark to fire a mind."

Lawrence Durrell

Today's Challenge

List ten motivators that you do to keep pushing through adversity or shortcomings?

DAY ONE HUNDRED-EIGHTEEN

Temptation

Definition

A thing or course of action that attracts or tempts someone

Repeat Out loud

Temptation arises from strength, vulnerability, circumstances, and a form of thought. I cannot yield to the negative temptation in my life by simply saying I will not give in to negative energy

Motivation

Temptation comes in all shapes and sizes with many colors and patterns. Feeding into negative cravings can feel like your best friend at times. Always there when you need them. Emotions can lead to decisions that may not have been made if in the right space of mind. No person is the same nor are their pains and coping methods. Judgment on others should never be cast when we all have vulnerable moments in our life. Overcoming those moments become a piece of our character and who we are on the inside and out.

1 Corinthians 10:13 NIV

No temptation has overtaken you except what is common to mankind. And God is faithful; he will not let you be tempted beyond what you can bear. But when you are tempted, he will also provide a way out so that you can endure it.

Today's Challenge

How can temptations harm you?

Do you have any temptations that can lead to negative outcomes?

How do you overcome such negative actions?

Transform

Definition

Change

Repeat Out loud

To transform into the King/Queen I want to become, I must first begin to be honest with myself, second orchestrate a plan to better myself, then execute it even through failure

Motivation

Transformation is not something that you look forward to and hope that it comes your way.

You actively work every day to change who you want to be.

Prime examples of transforming yourself or your brand come with consecutive GGrind every day to better who you are.

Let's look at someone who we all know, Jeff Bezos, owner of Amazon. He managed to convince 22 investors to back his new company Amazon in 1994.

Now in 2022 amazon is worth $438.118 billion with thousands of investors knocking to be a part of the vision daily.

Tyler Perry's dream didn't come true overnight. It took years of determination, struggle, adversity, and hardships before he got to where he is today.

For years Tyler Perry mentioned he struggled with paying rent and at a point in life became homeless. Sticking to his faith, and vision he not only bought the studio on the same blocks of Atlanta he was homeless and struggling but he is now worth 800 million, sharing his stories with the world, building communities, and following his dreams every moment of his life.

You are no different than the next person.

You have been blessed to be born which is more than enough.

Your story is now

Keep Going

Today's Challenge

List truthfully what characteristics you feel are a hindrance to your growth

Explain how you will better those characteristics

Definition

An end or final part or stage of something.

Repeat Out loud

Finishing is a success all alone, however, finishing does not require success to be the outcome. When I commit to a goal, finishing shows my character and who I am to others regardless of the outcome.

Whenever I feel like the challenge or task at hand is overwhelming it is okay to take a step back knowing I am going to approach the next, to go at it smarter and harder.

Motivation

Today, write these steps down on two small pieces of paper. We will finish everything to the best of our abilities every time we embark on any journey in our life

1. Only embark on stuff you're passionate about

2. Plan everything you will need to execute your goal

3. Budget your time and energy

4. Remember it is okay to make mistakes, for we are not perfect.

5. Your word is your bond, stay strong, and be dedicated to your vision.

6. Enjoy the process's ups and downs by all means.

7. Track your progress, and look how far you came.

8. Celebrate what you've done so far.

9. Keep Educating yourself on how you can get better at achieving your visions.

10. Grind, Pray, Elevate, you got this.

Today's Challenge

Why did I start if I'm not going to finish?

Does failing to finish a task or goal make you feel emotions of sadness, anger, or incompleteness?

How can you battle that feeling of not being able to finish?

List out all your goals creating a checklist from start to finish on how you will accomplish them.

After accomplishing your goals write how you feel about accomplishing them, where you would be if not accomplishing them and what steps you took to accomplish your goals?

Not Good Enough

Definition

You or someone not being satisfied with what something or someone has done or offered you.

Repeat Out loud

If I am making an effort to become a better me every day, my happiness and peace will come, just continue to GGrind twice as hard.

Motivation

1. You were chosen to exist. Whether by God or what you may, or may not place your faith in, you are here. You have a purpose.

2. You are always good enough because you have something no one else has to offer. No one else can compare to you.

3. Someone out there loves you. You may feel as if you are all alone physically or mentally but stop that thought process today. Sometimes different metrics in life can make us not tell those we love that we love and cherish the good in them including the negative in them

4. You are good enough because you dare to keep going every day through all the adversities.

5. You understood that you were worth more than the way you were treated. You learned to move on.

6. You've become aware of the people who want to stay in your life and those who need to be removed from your life peacefully...

7. You are learning how to forgive

8. You are good enough because you have let your emotions control your actions at times, but humbling as everyone in the world is different communication will be different. You've sat down and drowned in yourself and truly known what it means to be human.

9. You think outside of the box.

10. You are good enough, although you may be in a hard place right now, or maybe you're just having a rough day, you know that things will get better if you find the positive in all situations.

Today's Challenge

Write a list of twenty reasons you are good enough to achieve anything you set forth!

Take your time

Definition

Something that causes laughter; is a source of fun, amusement, or derision.

Repeat Out loud

Laugh, I will not be afraid to find laughter on both sides of the spectrum. Laughing is a healthy way to remain at peace

Motivation

Life is serious but not to the point where you can't enjoy a good laugh. I'm not asking you to become Kevin Hart but to merely create a pattern of laughing that sparks fire in the soul. Feeling good about yourself and comfortable expressing yourself is the ultimate first step in controlling who you are.

"Don't take life too seriously. You'll never get out of it alive."

Elbert Hubbard

Today's Challenge

When was the last time you laughed like it was the first time?

What makes you laugh, or smile?

Love

Definition

An intense feeling of deep affection or great interest

Repeat Out loud

Love is beauty on a double-edged sword. Precise and sharp to the finest detail. Love can create everlasting bonds. Never smooth love can also throw Cleveland size potholes at you as well. I must remain gentle with my heart and clear with my mind.

Motivation

Love can alter thinking and actions in many ways, and even change some actions greatly. Enjoying the nature of love can become life-changing. Moments where love can feel so right and then possible moments where that same love can lead to points of devastation. Love is gentle and here to stay. What we do with her is what's important

You must first love yourself properly
Love your family endlessly

Treat your friends and even foes with pure love

Today's Challenge

What do you think of yourself? Positive and negative thoughts?

Toss all the negative thoughts of yourself out the window. Begin to love every bit of who you are.

Invent

Definition

Create or design something that has not existed before; be the originator of it.

Repeat Out loud

Process, analyze the needs of humanity and invent new creations for the world to embrace.

Motivation

Get the brain going with some brain teasers you can do with all ages, friends, family, neighbors, and whoever you may hold a conversation with today.

To invent or be the originator of anything you need to open your mind and have a great imagination.

1.) Before Mount Everest was discovered, what was the tallest mountain in the world?

2.) What is a common eleven-letter word always spelled incorrectly?

3.) What do you find in the middle of nowhere?

ANSWERS: 1.) Mount Everest. 2.) Incorrectly. 3.) The letter H.

Today's Challenge

What changes does our world need that you see?

How can you create something or become someone who can direct those changes you see?

Act

Definition

Take action; do something.

Repeat Out loud

There is no constructive action without some form of thought. No stalling or telling myself I cannot make it happen. I will think, plan, and then act

Motivation

Twenty years from now you will be more disappointed by the things that you didn't do than by the ones you did do. So, throw off the bowlines. Sail away from the safe harbor. Catch the trade winds in your sails. Explore. Dream. Discover.

H. Jackson Brown

Your beliefs become your thoughts, Your thoughts become your words, Your words become your actions, Your actions become your habits, Your habits become your values, Your values become your destiny.

Gandhi

Today's Challenge

Today is the day of action. Tell yourself you can overcome and make it happen

Start now by acting on three things you have thought about doing but just didn't get to do yet.

Confident

Definition

A feeling of self-assurance that arises from one's appreciation of one's abilities or qualities.

Repeat Out loud

When I begin to see my true worth, I will begin to stray away from those who don't! Facing my fears builds confidence, completing goals gains confidence, building a mindset of every day is a better day than not building at all. Regardless of circumstance creates the confidence to be the best person you can be every single day

Motivation

Did you know that Dr. Seuss was rejected by nearly 27 publishers early in his career?

One of the most noteworthy authors of children's literature and whose work will probably live on for another 100 years and more.

He believed in his creativity and what he had to share with the world. Never allowing failure or rejection to completely take him away from his vision. With his confidence, determination, and persistence Dr. Seuss was able to illustrate the childhood of millions of kids all around the world.

Today's Challenge

Become confident in your abilities and knowledge. You can achieve all you desire

Today will be the day you face your fears.

Today, try to do something you have never done before!

There is a first time for everything

Embrace who you are and enjoy your time breaking free of any restraints

Proclaim

Definition

Declare something one considers important with due emphasis.

Repeat Out loud

I will proclaim positive light in all my daily affairs, seeking honesty with all my actions and living now for the future I want tomorrow

Motivation

There is a ripple effect to the gospel that's inevitable. There's a ripple effect to true grace. It doesn't lead us to only sit and contemplate what happened to us. It leads us to proclaim what's happened to us—and what can happen to anybody and everybody on the planet.

Louie Giglio

Today's Challenge

Proclaim your truths now

How do you truly feel about everything in your life?

How do you want to feel?

How can you stand on your faith and word regardless of the scenario in your life?

Presence

Definition

A person or thing that exists or is present in a place

Repeat Out loud

Simply, my presence acts like a million presents. Being there in the moment speaks volumes

Motivation

We never know when we will never see someone again or when we will see someone for the last time. The Most High puts people in our lives for reasons that may be uncertain at those exact moments. Those reasons become blessings and some become lessons that we should cherish.

The ones around us who care and love us for who we are should be who we spend time with, share laughs, create memories that will last beyond a lifetime and nothing else can do that for you but being in the presence.

Today's Challenge

Let's open our eyes, the world is so beautiful and far too often we do not get to enjoy just being here.

Today take a nature walk

No electronics, just you and the world for at least an hour

Enjoy being outside, looking at the sky, breathing the air, seeing trees, water and animals cross your face

Definition

An intention or decision about what one is going to do.

Repeat Out loud

For any goal to be met, I must first take those ideas, thoughts, emotions, dreams, actions, or physical creations that rest on a small parcel within my mind and put them until I properly plan and align my dreams.

Motivation

Define your goal

- Establish a timeline from start to finish

- Create a written plan describing The Who, What, Where, Why, and When of your plan

- Outline the positive and negative outcomes of your goal

- Analyze your action plan to include emergencies and moments of uncertainty.

- List proper channels to help you achieve your goal(s)

- Never Quit
- Ask for help if needed
- Learn from your actions to achieve your goal

- Celebrate the progress of your success whether success or failure

Today's Challenge

Write your goal for the week

Even if you do not accomplish the overall goal look at how much further you have come

Thrive

Definition

Prosper; flourish.

Repeat Out loud

All Situations will not be as I make them but I will thrive in all situations. The Most High has invested in me; powers of wisdom, courageousness, strength, and everlasting faith. I will think outside the box to thrive when the circumstances are not in my favor and when in my favor with grace and gratitude humbly accept all I deserve.

Motivation

Some of the most precious things and people on this earth and beyond earth's spectrum have undergone enormous amounts of trials and tribulations having to thrive under the pressures.

Think of some people who you have heard stories of or know that learned how to survive and thrive with the odds against them.

You can thrive in any circumstances by placing faith in your higher power and yourself; you are already winning.

Our deepest battles become our strongest triumphs. Failure, pain, and struggle create opportunities and success is the repeated effort executed daily to better oneself.

Today's Challenge

The way the old saying goes; pressure makes diamonds or can bust pipes

List ten scenarios where you feel as if you thrived under pressure and why?

What traits do you pull out of your spirit to lead you to success in those scenarios?

Can you thrive in every moment of your life even when negativity is knocking on your room door?

Test

Definition

Reveal the strengths or capabilities of someone or something by putting them under strain.

Repeat Out loud

My responses to all that I have in front of me and all that is to come are my answers to the test. Previous results do not define who I am but merely show where I can improve or continue to better myself.

Motivation

Tests in this context aren't the normal standardized test we remember from grade school where we learn concepts and then we take a test to see how good of a memory we have.

Tests are developed every single day with my daily actions, thoughts, relationships, words, and how we process situations in our lives are the true tests.

Today's Challenge

Challenge ten friends today is the #DestinationSerenityChallenge

Record a video of you overcoming an obstacle or speaking light on a recent circumstance where you overcame something that you were struggling with.

Test and challenge your peers to overcome all their obstacles as well. Have them create a video just as you did; speaking to their audience on the test and how they overcame obstacles within their life tagging #DestinationSerenityChallenge

Please feel free to tag me in your video on social media for a repost @GrindTime_ DQ and if you could please shout out at the Destination Serenity Book Series thank you so much.

Definition

Raise the level of; improve or lift to a higher power

Repeat Out loud

I will uplift those around me even when my spirit is low and I will always continue to uplift myself knowing there's always light at the end of the tunnel

Motivation

Have you ever thought about why they call today the present? Why is every single day we wake up a blessing?

The gift of today can be exchanged for laughter, happiness, love, friendship, family, abundance, and growth for ourselves, our communities, and those all around.

It's the journey we take to find our serenity, not the destination of peace, that counts.

"Try to be a rainbow in someone else's cloud"

Maya Angelou

Today's Challenge

For the entire day, no matter what the scenario is or what is said to you, think of the positives through everything.

At the end of the day write how thinking of the positives even though hard points and adversities made you feel.

Definition

Great energy or enthusiasm in pursuit of a cause or an objective.

Repeat Out loud

I want to be someone who changes the lives of those around me, including myself for the better. I want to be happy and stress-free. I must operate my life with zeal and intentions knowing I will rise above the tide.

Motivation

It is not hard to harp on the negative surrounding you, it almost becomes natural to allow stress and emotions to dictate how we operate throughout the day. When we break it down, we look at negativity for what it truly is. Forced into TV, Music, News, Politics, Finances and our everyday lives, negativity speaks at a constantly higher frequency always wanting to be heard. Where those little positive comments or actions are often trumped daily due to the volume with which negativity is trying to reach.

There are 1140 minutes in one day. Allowing even 10 of those minutes to reshape your state of mind and actions is to bring those unwanted energies closer to your anatomy. Time is precious and waits for no one. Live life timeless, free, and keep positive even when the negatives may tend to outweigh.

Today's Challenge

Those 1140 minutes a day can be cut short for anyone at any time. To be at peace with myself is to be aware and conscious of the world and those around me.

Today let's get excited about who we are

Hype yourself up all-day

Look at you

True Royalty

Your mind, spirit, movement, soul all speak volumes

Keep elevating you are doing your thing

Communicate

Definition

Conveying or sharing ideas, information, news, and feelings. There are many forms of communication

Repeat Out loud

Communication comes from all around me.

When communicating with people I must listen, and analyze what is being communicated to me.

Essential to the life I am living, communication is extremely vital and an important key to my life. Over half of the communication, I will be a part of in my life will be nonverbal.

Motivation

The single biggest problem in communication is the illusion that it has taken place.

George Bernard Shaw

Half the world is composed of people who have something to say and can't, and the other half who have nothing to say and keep on saying it.

Robert Frost

You never know when a moment in a few sincere words can have an impact on my life

Zig Ziglar

Today's Challenge

Compliment 25 people in the next seven days

How does randomly complimenting someone make you feel?

Challenge four friends or family members you have seen really thriving and bettering themselves daily on social media tag #DestinationSerenityChallenge and your chosen persons in a post complimenting every person, explaining why they are phenomenal, and telling them to do the same in a video tagging their loved ones.

The power of positivity when we are communicating becomes so vital to the overall development of our life.

Far too often we believe tough love is the only love and gather negative comment after negative comment not knowing that reassurance sometimes can change the projectile of how we move whether mentally or physically.

Communication is a connection beyond words, reading the emotions and nonverbal communication of another person increases understanding and elevates relationships.

Thorough listening and responses come without thought and communication is the key to operating life.

Faith

Definition

Complete trust or confidence in someone or something

Repeat Out loud

Faith is felt from within and much bigger than just me, surrounding me at my lowest point and most prestigious moments. Faith is where strength comes from when I feel like I have nothing left in the tank. Faith allows hope, acceptance, and happiness to stream when the plague has overcome the horizon.

Motivation

Now faith is the substance of things hoped for, the evidence of things not seen

Hebrews 11:1 (KJV)

Today's Challenge

Give thanks today, you were not the only person you needed to get to where you are today!

Even if you are completely alone there is always somebody in your corner wanting to see your growth.

From the man that opened the door for you and said have a blessed day to the lady that made sure you and your family could get food before the store closed.

No matter how big or small the deed was, it made your life less complicated at that moment and helped aid you in your journey.

Most importantly, give thanks to the higher power you believe in. Some moments in our life can't be explained by a man or woman. Let's give thanks for those times

You are Greatness

Meaningful

Definition

Having a serious, important, or useful quality or purpose.

Repeat Out loud

I must know what is important to me and I pursue just that. And along the way cherish life and the people around me spreading my knowledge to anyone willing to learn or even less fortunate than I am. Adding meaning to my life is simply adding love to my actions. Cherishing my purpoes and loving those around me.

Motivation

Learn to light a candle in the darkest moments of someone's life. Be the light that helps others see; it is what gives life its deepest significance.

Roy T. Bennett

The greatest challenge in life is to be our own person and accept that being different is a blessing and not a curse. A person who knows who they are lives a simple life by eliminating from their orbit anything that does not align with his or her overriding purpose and values. A person must be selective with their time and energy because both elements of life are limited.

Kilroy J. Oldster

Today's Challenge

What does meaningful mean to you?

What or who is meaningful in your life?

If you just won your own private island and could only take the five most meaningful resources or people, what and who would they be?

Why did you choose those resources or individuals?

Nurture

Definition

Care for and encourage the growth or development of someone or something.

Repeat Out loud

My soul will lead me to a path of nurturing others but never should I forget to nurture my own needs and wants.

Motivation

There are many differing viewpoints on nurture,

When we look at the theories behind nurturing, we get a few that become most common in all of our lives at one point.

First, being tough love or going through adversity after adversity will develop characteristics or can make us better and fit individuals in this world

Second, being super nice all the time, allowing someone to just push over you, and always being the yes person to someone will eventually lead to better individuals.

Don't get me wrong there are many situations where a push in the back, or a "You got this," even "Do this all on your own," are needed and vital. Along with being super supportive and that's it no strings or feelings attached

Tough love can become damaging mentally and possibly physically if done with any intent other than to better that person. Being super supportive can become damaging just as much, due to you not being honest, authentic, and not helping that person grow.

That is a piece of nurturing that many don't want to discuss, but we have to take the comments we don't want to hear just as much if not more than the ones we do like to hear.

When dealing with nurturing others we have to truly take in how that person communicates and learns.

Today's Challenge

Anger, hurt, pain, humiliation, fear, dread, confusion-all these emotions we choose. Do we hold on to our anger, our pain, and humiliation, and hit back, or do we strive to understand that we can do better?

Rosemary Altea

Optimistic

Definition

Hopeful and confident about the future.

Repeat Out loud

I know my future is filled with joy, mounds of success, tons of love, and laughter even when my current situation does not tell that same tale. I am optimistic about my wonderful future to come.

Motivation

Live your life knowing and being confident

When we wake up every morning, we reframe our mindset by asking each morning if we want to think negative or positive today?

Thank everyone and everything you are

thankful for

Look in the mirror and scream

"I am who I am, I am Great, Powerful Unstoppable, Unbreakable, I am legendary"

Dear Lord, in the battles we go through in life, We ask for a chance that's fair, A chance to equal our strides, A chance to do or dare, If we should win, Let it be by the code, With faith and honor held high, If we should lose, We'll stand by the road, and Cheer as the winners go by. Day by day, We get better and better, till we can't be beat,

Won't. Be. Beat.

1994   Nebraska   Cornhuskers
Championship Football Team

Today's Challenge

What are your wildest dreams?

Don't hold back, if every star is aligned what would you be doing, wearing, eating, driving, what would you even be?

Think well; preferably outside the box for this challenge

Definition

Feeling deep pleasure or satisfaction as a result of one's own achievements, qualities, or possessions or those of someone with whom one is closely associated.

Repeat Out loud

Always be proud of the person I am becoming I know every situation I have been through, has made me into the blessing I am today and will be tomorrow. I am proud of what I've been through where I've come from and who I am.

Motivation

Follow your passion. If you are not proud of what you do then you must focus your efforts.

Do not be scared to leave your comfort zone and challenge yourself.

Continue to always gain knowledge, practice your craft and be your biggest critique without negatively downgrading your progress.

Today's Challenge

It doesn't matter what it is, nor how small or big

Create a list of at least ten things you are proud of about yourself

Definition

Reinvigorate; give new strength or energy to yourself.

Repeat Out loud

It is important to refresh my mind and body as much as possible and to find my peace away from work and stress.

Motivation

Refreshing Your Mind and Increasing Productivity Tips

- Take breaks when you can during your day where you relax your mind and body.

- Quiet Your Thoughts. Try not to think of anything, blank your mind out

- Listen to your breathing and music that calms you not excites or makes you feel any way besides being relaxed. Try a new genre of music

- Take a Walk.

- Take a Break from social media.

Today's Challenge

Take a step away from social media, TV, Phones, Computers, and all the vitals that do not bring you ultimate peace daily for two hours today

Breath

Relax

Find your place of PEACE

Refresh your thoughts, gather your energy

Tell yourself you are GREAT with every chance you get

Advocate

Definition

A person who pleads on someone else's behalf; supports or recommends a particular cause or policy.

Repeat Out loud

I am an advocate for humans, our rights, our world, freedoms, dreams, our earth, and our journeys.

Motivation

We must understand that to be an advocate, mentor, or someone who likes to spread those simple gestures of positive faith, and energy does not require you to be perfect or carry no flaws.

The fact that we are not perfect and we do carry flaws along with lessons through life's challenges enables us to share our knowledge with others.

Today's Challenge

How can you help get involved in bettering those similar to you but not in the right position to overcome that jump?

Analyze

Definition

Examine, discover, and reveal methodically, and in detail the constitution or structure of something (especially information), typically for purposes of explanation and interpretation.

Repeat Out loud

I cannot be afraid to analyze my current situation. Analyzing the people, activities, and ways of living will allow me to always be true to myself and make me aware of the world around me, the people surrounding me, and know when a scenario fit who I am wanting to be or know that I need to walk the other direction a step away.

Motivation

When analyzing the people who surround you, do you feel as if you have a strong mind and a positively driven group of supporters?

Today's Challenge

Create a personal list of activities you like, your hobbies, what makes you happy, and where you find yourself most comfortable.

Carefully analyze how you spend your time, money, energy, and other resources.

Create a small list

What opportunities can you create from your current situations?

Purpose

Definition

One's intention or objective.

Repeat Out loud

My passions, peace, and happiness lie just in the bushes where my purpose lay and it is for me to act on my purpose and spread knowledge of my purpose to those not who might be unaware. When I am feeling unhappy or unsure of who I am and what I do I must reevaluate my purpose, my current set of daily goals in my current mindset

Motivation

If you can't figure out your purpose, figure out your passions. For your passion will lead you right into your purpose.

Bishop T.D. Jakes

It doesn't interest me what you do for a living, I want to know what you ache for, and if you dream of meeting your heart's longing.

Oriah

Today's Challenge

What do you like to do?

What are you naturally good at?

What changes would you make to the world if all your dreams come true?

Do you follow your heart?

Definition

Drive, push, or cause to move in a particular direction, typically forward

Repeat Out loud

I will use my adversities, struggles, and hardships to propel me through the skies

Motivation

The value of a moment is immeasurable. The power of just ONE moment can propel you to success and happiness or chain you to failure and misery.

Steve Maraboli

Imagine being at a place of complete peace, achieving those lifelong goals you have been grinding for after propelling past all the adversities you were faced with.

You Got This, Push Forward

Propel yourself beyond the farthest galaxy's horizons

Today's Challenge

Today is the day you will use all you are blessed with to achieve one goal for your future that you will completely conquer

Conquer your day!

Once you have completed your goal pat yourself on the back and celebrate your achievement.

Use that same energy and momentum to continue propelling through goals in your life.

Definition

Make available for use; supply.

Repeat Out loud

I will provide myself with the proper tools, knowledge, connections, and utensils to take advantage of every opportunity granted to me.

Motivation

The soul of a provider will always prevail. As you are willing to give instead of receiving; with that mindset, the Lord's favor will continue to be upon you and create internal peace within your life Until we know who we are and why we are here, no amount of success, fame, money, or pleasure will provide much satisfaction.

James C. Dobson

To get rid of a spiritual problem, we need to pull it up by its spiritual root. To pull up roots, we're going to have to be willing to get our hands dirty, to make some sacrifices that provide long-term benefits instead of short-term, refinanced gains. God is willing to help us, to provide the tools we need to weed out those areas where our desire for money is spoiling our fruit of the Spirit.

Craig Groeschel

Today's Challenge

List the characteristics of a Provider?

List the positive and negatives characteristics of being a provider or giver

List the benefits of giving rather than only receiving

DAY ONE HUNDRED-FOURTY SIX

Pursue

Definition

Seek to attain or accomplish a goal over a long period.

Repeat Out loud

I have to remain very conscious of what I pursue as all my desires, passions, wants, needs, and everything in between becoming a part of my pursuit of conquering who I am mentally and physically

Motivation

Pursue a passion

Find opportunities to turn these passions into a way to make additional income or pursue a full-time career.

Depending on your passion, you may also join relevant classes and organizations or attend events that allow you to meet and develop connections with like-minded people and even find yourself in a position to give back to those less fortunate.

Explore your interests, learn the unknown, contest injustice and keep pursuing who you are.

Today's Challenge

What Challenges will you give yourself today?

Write 3 challenges you will give yourself today and then after attempting each one, write exactly how you did and how you feel?

Definition

To look at, discover, and comprehend the meaning of written or printed matter by mentally interpreting the characters or symbols of which it is composed.

Repeat Out loud

Read between the lines to understand what is meant to be and what is not meant to be in my life. I will begin to sharpen my mind by reading more materials that deliver knowledge to me on higher levels. I will read over the material as reading is essential to my prestigious development in life, mentally and physically.

Motivation

According to the Bureau of Labor Statistics, People aged 15–44 in the US spend 10 minutes or less per day reading.

43 million Adults in the US possess low literacy skills according to a program for the International Assessment of Adult Competence meaning 1 out of 5 have difficult c ompleting task that require comparing and contrasting information, paraphrasing, or making decisions requires reading of some sort.

Reading for as little as 30 minutes a week can produce greater life satisfaction according to Quick Reads as well as significantly broadening one's general knowledge.

In a study from the University of Liverpool, respondents who described themselves as readers were 10% more likely than non-readers to report adequate levels of self-esteem and a study from the University of Minnesota states reading reduces stress by up to 68%.

Many Neurologists, if not all, will tell you that reading is mentally stimulating and could help extremely to reduce mental decline in old age

Reading can greatly impact your mental and physical well-being positively or negatively.

Today's Challenge

How many books have you read this month?

Do you read over contracts, and policies, in their full entirety?

What is the importance of reading?

How can you make reading more enjoyable for you?

Definition

Make or become less tense or anxious.

Repeat Out loud

Today I will make a promise to myself that I will always prevail. Taking a step away to relax from everyday pressures can serve magnitudes of positive energy into my soul and body. I promise every day will not feel as if I am winning the lottery to my dreams but I do know every day is meant to be a day enjoying the life I am blessed to have and conquering my purpose on this earth. It will always be okay to not have it all figured out in one day. It will never be ok that I carry traits of jealousy or comparing one's level of success negatively. All of our paths are made especially for us. Knowing this is allowing me to move at my speed.

Motivation

Free your mind. Disentangle your mindset from what can set your mind from your true purpose. Dare when you have to. Enjoy when it is a must. Relax when there is the need to, but don't spend the time. Don't let wealth be a hindrance to fulfilling your true you. Don't let poverty captivate you. Don't let the environment engulf your true purpose; if possible, flee to be free to dare. We all have excuses. Yourself is the most important factor in fulfilling your true you. Free your mind!!!

Ernest Agyemang Yeboah

Today's Challenge

Go to your peaceful place today for 30 minutes to an hour and write down all your thoughts

Once you are finished writing, release every single thought, slide your eyelids down, and just focus on breathing.

Have you noticed how it was okay to take a step away from everything on your mind and just relax?

How did clearing your mind feel?

Renew

Definition

Give fresh life or strength to; revive.

Repeat Out loud

I will train my mind to be stronger than my emotions. The best way to renew me is to renew my spirit.

Motivation

And be not conformed to this world: but be ye transformed by the renewing of your mind, that ye may prove what is that good, and acceptable, and perfect, will of God.

Romans 12:2 KJV

Looking at life from even the most scientific perspective; our body is constantly changing, cells, limbs, and senses we all are building daily. We are never the same person as we were yesterday, and renewal is filled with ample room for growth. Renew positive ways of thinking, living, and communicating continuously building on to your pyramid.

Today's Challenge

Today we are all Artists

Top shelf world-renowned award-winning artists if you ask me.

Paint on a canvas your mind's happiest thought

Post all pictures to social media tagging @GrindTime_DQ and #Destination SerenityChallenge

Today when you get some time say a prayer thanking you for all you have and those still to come

Become

Definition

Begin to be

Repeat Out loud

I will become what I set out to become. I will become the best me every day, I will become someone who never takes less than my worth.

Motivation

Who do you want to become?

What legacy do you want?

What do you want those who look up to you to become?

What will your family's name become?

Today's Challenge

Time to build on the things we sometimes want to build on, those negative habits or traits

Ask about seven people you are close with to share sometimes about you and write down three anecdotes when you were at your best and three when you were at your worse

Analyze everyone's answers

Write a web list of your actions from the stories shared about you; splitting the negatives and positives?

Now how can you continue to better your positives and how can you work on those negatives?

What changes will you make to become a better person?

Retain

Definition

Absorb and continue to hold; keep in one's memory

Repeat Out loud

If I continue to retain the feelings, skills, traits, and knowledge that I have learned through trial and error, research, in person, and from knowledgeable sources applying these points of knowledge to my everyday GGrind I can create opportunities that I never knew would be possible.

Motivation

Adifficult time can be more readily endured if we retain the conviction that our existence holds a purpose - a cause to pursue, a person to love, a goal to achieve.

John Maxwell

Today's Challenge

What are some things that you learned as a child that you still do to this day?

What processes, habits, or traits help you learn and remember what you have learned better?

Believe

Definition

Accepting something as true; feeling sure of the truth or having faith in it.

Repeat Out loud

I believe my mind, body, spirit, and soul will lead me to the right destiny. I am a believer that this world and the Most High can work miracles when I keep positive faith and a dedicated grind

Motivation

Anything is possible when you believe in yourself

For me growing up and believing in myself meant overcoming the bruising words of discouragement. I felt being called retarded, being told I'm not going to make it in life, people close to me were saying I would be dead, some trying to joke in say I'm fat, even those close to me or in positions to further my life and visions said I wasn't good enough.

Hardships of my father being killed, getting kicked out of school every other week, dealing with anger, almost losing my life to gun violence and so many more trials knocking my vision.

By believing in myself and my gifts from God, I was able to keep striving, break barriers, accomplish so many goals, and take life head-on.

I graduated from college and became a serial entrepreneur, loving father, family member, caring friend, mentor, community leader, musical engineer, and investor with so many more goals to accomplish.

That's a piece of my story.

There are millions of stories around the world, we all are unique including you.

What's your story?

Today's Challenge

What do you stand for?

Do you believe your visions match your daily actions?

Nature

Definition

The phenomena of the physical world collectively, including plants, animals, the landscape, and other features and products of the earth, as opposed to humans or human creations.

Repeat Out loud

Nature's process gradually works its graces creating beautiful mountain tops, parcels of grass greener than that of Granny Smith's green apples, sparks of land no human can define, and with no rush to the natural process of accomplishment. If I continue to match my mindset to the unique beauties of the world I then can grow peacefully without time or worry.

Motivation

Today we will become Photographers and Videographers with our minds enjoying the beauties of the world that are not man-made.

Take a two-hour walk today simply to enjoy the natural beauty of Mother Nature. Look at new flowers, adventure further into the woods, and look for animals high and low.

Take pictures and videos with your mind or on your phone, whichever you prefer.

Enjoy your time with one of the most precious gifts gifted to us every day.

Today's Challenge

What benefits can nature do for you?

Care

Definition

Feel concerned or interested; attach importance to something.

Repeat Out loud

I will always care for those who care about my well-being and overall growth in life. I must make a strong note to never forget that if I do not care for myself first, I cannot care for anyone else properly. So, every day I will be progressively working to better myself daily.

Motivation

One person caring about another person is life's greatest value

Jim Rohn

Self care is giving the world the best of you instead, of what's left of you

Katie Reed

Today's Challenge

Create a short story that describes a scene where caring for yourself allowed you to care for others around you

Tag ten friends to do the same and don't forget to #DestinationSerenityChallenge

Definition

Make suffering, deficiency, or a problem less severe.

Repeat Out loud

I am letting go of all my past emotions, encounters, and negative energies. I will alleviate my mind from negativity

Motivation

Relief is a great feeling.

A time to learn and reevaluate

It's the emotional and physical reward we receive from our bodies upon the alleviation of pain, grind, pressure, and/or struggle.

"Use your moment of relief well."

Vera Nazarian

Today's Challenge

Would a step back in which you remove yourself from your situation, or what you are dealing with at the moment be a regression, or is it an opportunity to regroup, start over, and move in a different direction?

Explain the rationale of your belief in the above question? There is no wrong answer, just room to explain the logic behind your thinking.

Definition

Giving strength or energy to something.

Repeat Out loud

Invigorate my Grind to help me double my income, and build who I am as a person

Motivation

It's only by taking myself away from clutter and distraction that I can begin to hear something out of earshot and recall that listening is much more invigorating than giving voice to all the thoughts and prejudices that keep me company twenty-four hours a day.

Pico Iyer

The soul, cramped among the petty vexations of Earth, needs to keep its windows constantly open to the invigorating air of large and free ideas: and what thought is so grand as that of an ever-present God, in whom all that is vital in humanity breathes and grows?

Lucy Larcom

Today's Challenge

What energizes you?

DAY ONE HUNDRED-FIFTY SEVEN

Diamond

Definition

A precious stone consisting of a clear and colorless crystalline form of pure carbon, the hardest naturally occurring substance. Its sheer strength has earned its associations with invincibility, courage, and strength among humans.

Repeat Out loud

I am a prize diamond covered in the deep pits of dirt, sludge, and pressure compacted on top of each other. Regardless of what mud I am dragged through, who spills false truths of who I am, or what situations and outcomes do not go in my favor, I am that, Diamond. One quick rinsing off the dirt, grime, mud, and unequal soil shining I begin to walk with a magnificent gleam of power, inspiration, and knowledge.

Motivation

Without pressure, and struggling through thousands of pounds of mud, rocks, and debris, a diamond never becomes that beautiful crystal shining for the world to see that we all know.

Similar to you without any pressure, or adversity you don't learn how to deal with shortcomings making you stronger. We need the dirt to almost cover us up so we know who we are, what's good for us, who may not be good for us, we begin to breakdown the properties trying to destroy us and shine bright like a diamond

Today's Challenge

Write "I am" 25 times and describe who you are positively using 25 sentences, phrases, emojis, drawings, words whatever you find best fit to describe who you are?

Guide

Definition

Direct or influence the course of action of someone or something. A person, or resource who advises or shows the way to others.

Repeat Out loud

I know there will be times that are carry the most urgent consequences and then times when the moments are prosperous. I will guide myself with the proper tools throughout my life continuously building my knowledge, faith, and diligence making it happen day by day.

Motivation

"Don't be ashamed to let your conscience be your" guide.

Aaron Neville

"The heart, not the head, must be the guide."

Arthur Erickson

"Faith is the light that guides you through the darkness"

Today's Challenge

List ten positive outlets you have in your life rather a place or person where can you go for guidance or to regain your guidance

Definition

Stop or discontinue an action or activity.

Repeat Out loud

Not finishing anything can leave an empty void deep inside of me if it is truly something I should have finished and would not have harmed myself or who I am then I have to note every challenge given to me as one that I will finish what I have started

Motivation

Quitting has two sides

The first one is quitting because you feel as if something or somebody is not for you or quitting because you can't or won't do it anymore.

Learning how to walk away from people, and situations can be one of the hardest things to do, however quitting unhealthy relationships and actions can lead to a better you.

If you are quitting because you feel as if you can't go anymore, or just because you do not feel like doing something or dealing with somebody you are creating bad habits. Quitting before you have accomplished the goal leaves you on the same playing field versus learning, and striving through the adversity pushing it to the limits. You never know when your breakthrough is coming don't start knocking down the walls just to have five more swings and quit. Think it is always too early to quit. You may struggle but you will never quit.

"One of the most common causes of failure is the habit of quitting when one is overtaken by temporary defeat."

Napoleon Hill

Today's Challenge

Tag 20 friends and #Destination SerenityChallenge

Create a video of you explaining a goal you have created no matter how big or small it may be to you and document your progress.

"Some individuals quit due to slow progress. Never grasping the fact that slow progress is still progress."

Flourish

Definition

Grow or develop in a healthy or vigorous way

Repeat Out loud

Flourish beyond the opposition's action plan for my life. I'm taking off nothing but positivity leading my way

Motivation

"As a flower can't bloom without sunshine so a life can't flourish without love."

Debasish Mridha, MD

"If beautiful lilies bloom in ugly waters, you too can blossom in ugly situations."

Matshona Dhliwayo

You will flourish with everything you do, keep your faith, stay persistent, pray, plan, grind and execute.

Experience your very best life. Find peace, create blessings, and grow your maturity level. Make this life we live precious, for every second, we are blessed to be able to breathe.

Today's Challenge

Imagine you have already made your visions come to light, and you are now very successful, happy, and wealthy.

How will you handle your success?

How will you continue striving to accomplish more goals now that you have accomplished your original visions?

DAY ONE HUNDRED-SIXTY ONE

Definition

Do honor or credit to someone or something by one's presence; courteousgoodwill; simple elegance of movement.

Repeat Out loud

No one has my back like my God. Giving grace and thanks to the Most High allows me to take the burden of everyday pressures off myself completely and share that load. My belief is my belief, my highest power is what keeps me going and I am blessed to be here. Grace, faith, persistence, and determination will always place me on a path to prevail.

Motivation

But by the grace of God, I am what I am: and his grace which was bestowed upon me was not in vain; but I laboured more abundantly than they all: yet not I, but the grace of God which was with me.

1 Corinthians 15:10 (KJV)

Today's Challenge

No publicizing your good deed.

Today, if you have a few extra dollars, buy lunch for somebody random you do not know...

DAY ONE HUNDRED-SIXTY TWO

Definition

Having or showing a friendly, generous, and considerate nature; a group of people or things; character

Repeat Out loud

I'll look to always spread positive energy, good vibes, and be kind to those around me and myself. When I wake up, I am blessed and that is the same for everyone else around me. Who I am when no one is looking builds who I am when everyone is looking.

Motivation

Being kind comes in many forms, and far too often we get caught in our own lives, egos, and minds not worrying about those around us or even ourselves at times.

One act of kindness can change the life of not only who you are helping, but those around you, and yourself.

As a young child, my mother and god grandmother would take me to feed the homeless. Always telling me no matter what we are going through in life somebody always has it much worse, but still, we are not to discredit our own struggles.

One gesture, comment, and action of good faith can lead to a lifetime bond of security, happiness, confidence, and growth.

A story that built my character, and still to this day I can never forget how good my actions made me feel. I was often known as the kid in school with all the friends, a class clown, and labeled the troublemaker. Teachers didn't expect too much good coming from me, however, that was always their judgment of who I really was.

The school had just let out all the kids, and we were on our way to the auditorium for our after-school program. I was racing down the halls, and walking into the room, more than 20 kids were laughing, pointing, and talking about one of my good friends who also happens to be Autistic.

Shamed and embarrassed my friend sat in the corner crying as these kids belittled him repeatedly.

Not entertaining any of the bullying, I pushed through the crowd of people poured water on my pants and splashed a cup of water on another student, told everyone to stop laughing, and sat next to my friend playing Connect Four for the next 2 hours sharing laughs and happiness.

Seeing those tears and that pain turned into a smile, and laughter that overtook my friend's heart warmed my heart, and all the teachers who labeled me a troublemaker, started crying happy tears hugging me.

The power of kindness is extremely vital.

Today's Challenge

The countdown starts now challenge your friends and family we have another #DestinationSerenityChallenge

Starting today, speak 200 kind words in a month about yourself and those around you during your day for the next 30 days, afterward, write down how being kind daily changes your mindset, and actions.

Heal

Definition

To become healthy, correct or put right

Repeat Out loud

Healing is essential to the soul, mind, body, and spirit. It might be times when healing is the least desirable thought in my mind. I will heal many times in my life from relationships, social life, and professional reasons, adding to many of life's twisted plot, which twists to the extent where healing will become an important tool to reclaiming my mind and actions onto my path of peace, happiness, and fulfillment.

Motivation

Visualizing yourself in a relaxing, positive space can help soothe your body and ease your mind.

Recollect and tell yourself it will always be okay; God doesn't give you battles you cannot handle.

You are a leader, the challenges you have been vested with in life are there because you are strong enough to flourish through all the adversity. Your testimony empowers the souls of all around you.

Poor mental healing can lead to mental deterioration and physical overload. I have personally seen NFL Football players break down and check into psychiatric centers, some of the strongest women snap to the point of almost no return. Destruction can occur in a split second, lives can be tarnished, and relationships are broken. We are living in an era of watching children publicly losing their life because of a decision made within three seconds.

We need to know it is always okay to reload, we are not perfect and this life we live is being shared with a higher power that we can lean on at any time.

We can heal from all with the right faith, mind, and grind

Today's Challenge

Why is it important to heal?

How do you heal yourself, finding your peace of mind after hardship?

Definition

Humility is the virtue of being humble and not holding any excessive feeling of pride.

Repeat Out loud

The driven purpose in why I operate with humility is not to think of myself less but to begin to think of others more. I've learned to treat the most poverty-stricken man on the street asking for change with the same respect I would treat someone who I value the utmost. At any given moment we can easily switch places transforming reality as we know it.

Motivation

"Humility isn't denying your strengths; it's being honest about your weaknesses."

Rick Warren

"Just knowing you don't have the answers is a recipe for humility, openness, acceptance, forgiveness, and an eagerness to learn - and those are all good things."

Dick Van Dyke

"Have more humility. Remember you don't know the limits of your own abilities. Successful or not, if you keep pushing beyond yourself, you will enrich your own life--and maybe even please a few strangers."

A. L. Kennedy

Today's Challenge

List 30 ways you can help others then begin using these ways week by week to accomplish helping others.

What does being humble mean to you?

Name a time when you were humbled and how did that scene make you feel?

Elevate

Definition

To raise or lift someone or something to a higher position.

Repeat Out loud

Every day I vow to elevate my mind, body, spirit, and soul.

Motivation

Find a peaceful place today and take time to channel those vibrant energy waves and your inner peace positively.

Close your eyes

Begin to think about your current situation and imagine you accomplishing all of your goals and how.

Channel what makes you happy and smile

Allow yourself to sit with your eyes closed relaxed through this meditation process

Your Thoughts are powerful

,

Today's Challenge

What will you elevate in your life starting today?

Definition

Life is a characteristic that distinguishes physical entities that have biological processes capable of performing functions such as eating, metabolizing, excreting, breathing, moving, growing, reproducing, and responding to external stimuli.

Repeat Out loud

Why would I ever want to live a life anybody else lives?

The life that I have has been granted to me and designed just for me. Nobody else can live it

Motivation

Naturally, I've always felt as if I had a healing nature, being able to listen and put myself inside somebody else's shoes without judgment rather wanting to see the best from them and aid them beyond their pains. I elevate and spread positive words and actions to my people when they are doing good as well.

Having that caring nature, I believe God enacts a sturdy shell layered to help navigate and balance myself as well as those who I am speaking with through these storms. I have witnessed many people express to me their life wasn't worth living or living with regret and resentment. I've been a part of elevating people from situations where suicide became the only option for them.

Let's cherish life, celebrate all the good, small or big, enjoy the relationships you have, and continue to elevate beyond your wildest imaginations.

Use the lessons you have learned through life and within this journey. Pray every single moment you can. We are blessed to be here and for that reason, we smile. Remember the life we live is precious, we only get one.

"Character cannot be developed in ease and quiet. Only through experience of trial and suffering can the soul be strengthened, ambition inspired, and success achieved."

Helen Keller

Today's Challenge

What is life?

Explain in your own words

Substance

Definition

The most essential part of something; is the real or essential meaning; the subject matter of a text, speech, or work of art, especially as contrasted with the form or style in which it is presented.

Repeat Out loud

I will design a life of substance that creates happiness even when it feels there is none to give. Be proud of who I am even when the pride is conquered by shame. The substance is found through truths, caring, growth and passion.

Motivation

We must look for ways to be an active force in our own lives. We must take charge of our own destinies, design a life of substance, and truly begin to live our dreams.

Les Brown

Today's Challenge

What is a life filled with substance?

How do you become a person of substance in your life?

Definition

To undergo a continuous change; become or make more extensive.

Repeat Out loud

My expansion can only go as far as my focus, determination, and will

Motivation

Life shrinks or expands in proportion to one's courage

Anais Nin

We only know a tiny proportion of the complexity of the natural world. Wherever you look, there are still things we don't know about and don't understand. There are always new things to find out if you go looking for them.

David Attenborough

,

Today's Challenge

What constitutes your primary focus?

Does your focus add up to your intended goals and responsibilities?

If you did not expand our versions in this world, where would you be now, how would life as you know it, be different?

Subtract

Definition

Take Away

Repeat Out loud

Subtract all individuals from my life that are never positive. I will no longer place myself in harm or situations I do not feel comfortable about. I am done with the tools used in this world to harm my growth and creation.

Today I'll be subtracting all negativity from my life. Today I will subtract any excuses from my life.

Today is the day I subtract anything from my life that is not for the advancement, development, fulfillment, and happiness of who I am and who I am becoming.

Motivation

Growing up, mathematics was my favorite subject, and still is to this day I am a math head to the fullest.

Math is in everything we do in life; I would take many lessons from school and create my own life examples for them. This at the time was a good way for me to remember formulas, and specific details, not knowing that thirteen years later, I will be writing to you about my oddly unorthodox but beneficial method of learning that I have always used the life values from creating a sense of security for myself and now for you today.

The quick Math lesson for today is PEMDAS:

PEMDAS is the order of operations and rules which tells the correct sequence of steps for evaluating a mathematical expression from left to right; Parentheses, Exponents, Multiplication, Division, Addition, and Subtraction

This is the life lesson I've been going by since was a teenager

P- Put a Parentheses around everything and everyone you value

E- Do everything you need to do at an Exponential rate. Every moment you are blessed to be here, without comprising who you are to accomplish your vision.

M- Multiply the positive energy and vibes

D- Divide your life into chapters, and set goals for each.

A- Add more knowledge to your daily diet

S- Subtract anybody or anything that hinders who you are becoming

Today's Challenge

List the negativity you will be liminating from your life.

Pride

Definition

A feeling of deep pleasure or satisfaction derived from one's own achievements, the achievements of those with whom one is closely associated, or from qualities or possessions that are widely admired.

Repeat Out loud

My Pride should not come at the expense of others nor harm myself and those around me. Pride is a mysterious trap that can leave me with nothing if abused. I have pride in who I am, my friends, family, culture, and what I like and that's more than okay, I just won't let my pride blind me to those around me.

Motivation

Pride can be dangerously harmful, leaving you with results much different from being proud of who you are. Looking beneath someone leaves you vulnerable to the clouds above your head, causing you to miss so many vital points in situations where your pride is being overextended. Pride has killed many and humbled billions.

"It was pride that changed angels into devils; it is humility that turns people into angels."

St. Augustine

Today's Challenge

Do you let your pride overtake your thoughts and actions at times?

What's the difference between pride and arrogance?

How can you control your pride to also make sure you make the best, clear-cut, decisions?

List ten moments in life from all around you where someone's pride leads to their downfall?

Observe

Definition

To watch someone or something carefully and attentively.

Repeat Out loud

I sat back to observe my surroundings, those I come into contact with, businesses, politics, and world dilemmas, I begin to take note of all. I learn by the observation that these notes of observation are filed into my brain and labeled as wisdom.

Motivation

Without observation, the world would not be able to grow properly.

Today's Challenge

I challenge you to observe every conversation and action you are surrounded by today and at the end of the day write a list of the new traits and attributes you observed about someone or something that you didn't observe yesterday

Definition

Used with a possessive to emphasize that someone or something belongs to or relates to the person or thing mentioned; have something as one's own; possess. Admit or acknowledge that something is the case or that one feels a certain way.

Repeat Out loud

If I don't focus on my dreams and happiness, someone else's dreams, happiness, and passions are going to own my everyday life. If I do not do it for myself, I cannot expect someone else to do it for me. I'm owning who I am now, and building for my happiness and who I plan to be.

Motivation

Be yourself, own who you are, and never compromise for any situation or person on this earth.

"Infuse your life with action. Don't wait for it to happen. Make it happen. Make your own future. Make your own hope. Make your own love. And whatever your beliefs, honor your creator, not by passively waiting for grace to come down from upon high, but by doing what you can to make grace happen... yourself, right now, right down here on Earth."

Bradley Whitford

Today's Challenge

Look in the mirror and make a rap song or sing to yourself about why you are Greatness, and can't be stopped when you are in your zone

Enjoy being silly, and admiring who you are

Confidence is key

Write

Definition

Mark letters, words, or other symbols on a surface, typically paper, with a pen, pencil, or similar implement.

Repeat Out loud

Write everything, never stop writing, and always express yourself with a pen and a pad or even the note section of my phone. Writing can go a very long way in self-healing, developing, creating, expressing oneself, and sharpening one's mind.

Motivation

Write your story for every moment you are granted on this earth. God has blessed us with the ability to be who we want to be and do what we want to do.

We cannot take any time for granted, write your story as you are the author of a magical story.

"If there's a book that you want to read, but it hasn't been written yet, then you must write it."

Toni Morrison

Today's Challenge

Write every single day about your day, thoughts, goals, dreams, create stories, and turn your writing into your daily peace of mind.

Settle

Definition

Determined; decide on, or reach an agreement.

Repeat Out loud

The moment I settle for less than I deserve is the moment I begin a pattern of expecting less which is a bad habit

Motivation

I want to ask you an honest question. It may seem silly at first but let's give the question an honest shake.

Do you think a lion settles for being the biggest beast in the Jungle?

The short answer to that question has to be, "no way!"

Every single day a lion wakes up with the intent to grow who they are, grow its family, grow its hunting skills, and grow mentally to become the biggest beast in the jungle.

The moment the lion settles for less is the moment the lion becomes the prey, loses a cub, or ends up somewhere not eating because they settle for the vegetarian versus working for the Gazelle.

Today's Challenge

Have you ever settled for less?

How did it make you feel?

What can you do to prevent yourself from settling for less than you deserve?

DAY ONE HUNDRED-SEVENTY FIVE

Definition

Fly or rise high in the air; increase rapidly above the usual level

Repeat Out loud

The acceptance of just being comfortable can become harmful if I am not intriguing my happiness and sparking my passions. I am doing myself a disservice if I do not allow my visions to soar.

Motivation

Think of everything you possibly can allow your mind to soar, allow your body to soar, and make plans to travel the world more often.

Today is the day you challenge yourself concerning your life to always get better than yesterday

Daquian H. Williams   292

Today's Challenge

What stops you from achieving all your goals?

If anything is stopping you, how can you combat that situation to get you back towards achieving your goals?

Are you ready to let your mind soar and allow your body to follow through with actions?

Definition

Attempt or desire to obtain or achieve something.

Repeat Out loud

Seek knowledge at all times, seek happiness at all moments, seek my passions and dreams every moment I breathe, seek to build a stronger relationship with my higher power daily...

Motivation

"Ask, and it shall be given you; seek, and ye shall find; knock, and it shall be opened unto you."

Matthew 7:7 (KJV)

Seek respect, honor, love, wisdom, faith, not attention, destruction, and approval.

Today's Challenge

Today is your day to go outside your comfort zone and seek discomfort.

Do an activity or try something that you never would have tried in a million years.

How did you feel after accomplishing the new activity or trying something new?

Life is about continuously improving and evolving as a person; when we seek to thrive in uncomfortable situations, we ultimately build the courage, wisdom, and confidence to thrive in environments in which we are comfortable.

DAY ONE HUNDRED-SEVENTY SEVEN

Definition

Place or arrange something or someone in an order; An adjustment

Repeat Out loud

Align my actions with my intended goals, align my mind to compliment myself always. If I stray away from my paths, I will be sure to realign my thoughts and actions to match who I am and who I want to be.

Motivation

To be in alignment with your best self implies that all aspects of ourselves are in harmony.

You operate in different realms from your spiritual, emotional, intellectual, and physical being all in one body and mind.

When all aspects of yourself are operating to serve your highest good, you're in alignment. When those aspects of your life find you creating bad habits, excuses, wrongdoings, and being dishonest you are now needing to realign your mind, soul and body.

Align your mind, soul, and body to one another daily. As humans, we will get tired, feel overworked, undervalued, and less important and all of those are mental blocks leaving the mind.

You will win if you continue to grow your knowledge, elevate your grind and pray.

Today's Challenge

Are your actions aligned with your purposes?

When your mind and body are aligned how should you feel?

Create a list of how you will realign yourself whenever you feel as if you need your chakras reloaded?

Definition

Expressing regret for something that one has done wrong.

Repeat Out loud

Never should I allow pride to conquer my wrongdoings or those done against me. If I am wrong, I will use my strength to admit I am wrong and apologize to those affected. When a wrong has been done to me I will build the courage to accept forgiveness but never forget the lessons I have learned.

Motivation

We far too often take a lot of the sweet gems here on earth for granted; not realizing how short life is. From a young age, younger than seven years old, I already experienced the death of multiple family members. I can honestly say at age seven when I attended the first wedding, I had used those same styles of dress pants and shoes to attend several funerals. A few years down the road, as was I'm pushing towards my teenage years, I began to see friends and children in the neighborhood die from violence. Learning the value of life at a young age, always made me appreciate the life we have. We truly never know when today is the day our name will be called to those gates. This is why we have to cherish those we love dearly and never leave off on any negative note because we can never predict tomorrow's sunshine.

Humbling our minds to accept that life is precious is a great step to altering the mind to want to always get smarter, telling the body to always chase your passions and happiness, and communicating to the soul that love and peace are the answers to a positive and regret-free life.

Today's Challenge

We all are guilty of words and actions we are not proud of, today create a list of the people to whom you owe an apology for whatever the reason. Now, on that list create a second list of the people from your list of apologies that truly love and support you.

Apologize to everyone on that second list

Reevaluate everyone on that first list and ask yourself if they did you wrong or truly don't care about you.

This list will become your reference guide for those individuals you no longer care to give energy to.

Give Thanks

Definition

Express gratitude or show appreciation to or for something.

Repeat Out loud

Along with the lesson, I learned yesterday about accepting apologies and apologizing when I am wrong, giving thanks sits high on the list. Giving thanks to the Most High, those who do good for me, and even those who've done the most harm to me but teaching me valuable lessons on my journey are vital to the overall growth of my mind and physical being.

Motivation

Tell everyone you cherish and are grateful to have in your life thank you today

Send them a message or give them a call just saying how you are grateful for all that they have done for you and all that is to come of your relationship.

We will build on the more serious notes with being thankful but for this specific challenge let's speak on some of those small things to be thankful for.

Pick the funniest thing or person you are thankful for and why

Post on your social media tagging 15 friends including our page and add #DestinationSerenityChallenge

Example of my post

I am thankful for the water bill every single month because without it Lord knows how hot my daughter's morning breath can be and let me not mention my after-workout feet!!

#DestinationSerenityChallenge
@GrindTime_DQ

I challenge ... friends below to express what they are giving thanks too

Today's Challenge

Who and what am I thankful for?

What situations have humbled and taught me lessons in my life?

You

Definition

Used to refer to any person in general.

Repeat Out loud

I am truly royalty. I am me and no one can be who I am better than me. Every morning I wake, it becomes a blessing and now I have another day to experience my happiness and pursue my passions. I will always cherish myself and answer my needs.

Motivation

"However difficult l ife m ay s eem,there is always something you can do and succeed at."

-Stephen Hawking

Creating a vision board for your life can define and clearly direct your priorities while ranking them in the level of importance to you. Allowing you better prepared to set measurable goals and success.

What are the things you stand for?

What are your strongest beliefs?

How do you want to live your life?

How do you want to define yourself?

What words do you want to live by?

Where do you see yourself in the next ten years?

This is the start of your vision board, continuing every day working to accomplish your goals and looking over your boards to make any updates along with breaking down goals more in-depth.

Your board is your vision

Today's Challenge

What have you learned about yourself this far through our journey?

Create a list of the good and the not so good (the bad) also known as the work to do pile

180 Days Strong

I am....

This last section will become a reminder of your everyday commitment to empowering your mind, spreading positivity, and bettering yourself and those around you!

Send all posts to @GrindTime_DQ or @GrindTimePublishingGroup attached with your email and your "I am" statement.

All of your "I am" statements will be publicly posted on all our platforms subject to your permission and you will become a part of the GrindTime Family giving you access to freebies, updates, events, and new releases.

I _____, am a _____

King or Queen

This world is here for me to learn, explore, enjoy, and spread love throughout.

I am in control of my feelings

I can accomplish all I set out to achieve
I believe in myself through struggle and triumph
I am grateful for all I have and all that is to come

This is a promise to me every day that I will allow all obstacles to help me grow.
Know there is only one me, I am special regardless of words, actions, and perceptions perceived by others around me.

Today I will make myself better and tomorrow I will become better than today!

I _____am striving for Better Days

Conclusion

Evolving

Those changes in your mindset and actions will start if they haven't already, and they will elevate who you are.

You are tapping into who you are, learning you can achieve all, and you are phenomenal.

Now that you have begun conditioning the mind to accept changes, create, expand and conquer. Remember that you control your destiny.

You have the essential tools to overcome adversities and challenges.

Your mind is now wrapped around following your visions with proper planning, praying, execution, and knowledge you cannot be stopped.

Let's get ready for Volume 3.

We will be conquering everything we set out to achieve.

GrindTime!

Thank you for reading, please do not forget to get Volume 3 we love you, and please endeavor to follow our page

GrindTime Publishing Group, and stay tuned for more.

We Are Family

I'll see you at the Cookout

About the Author

Never do we want to speak on the things that affect us the most but the older we get the more prominent it becomes to do just that in some form or fashion even if we cannot get the words out or have the actions to match our thought process.

Throughout the Destination Serenity Daily Interactive Series from Volumes 1 to Volumes 4, Daquian tells stories of his life throughout the journal. Reflecting on life and the values that his God, Mother, Grandparents, Family, and Friends instilled in him throughout life.

"From childhood deaths, and being told I would be dead or in jail, before I turned 16, dealing with anger, regret, negative feelings, and thoughts, I felt as if I couldn't control things, it became a toggle of trial after trial, some self-inflicted and others life's lessons and blessings in disguise. Concealing my emotions and not being myself led to not being able to give myself the best foot forward and that wasn't fair to who I am becoming or those around me who loved me.

There are situations in our life we deal with every day, or maybe once in a lifetime but they create long-lasting effects when caged can leave our minds to spoil like eight-week-old baby milk left on the side of the road.

Addressing our flaws and creating changes to build those flaws, keeping positive through all of life's ups and downs, knowing the power of our mind and words, while staying focused on our visions and plans, makes our growth of who we have become pure and we start to flourish in every direction.

Throughout my life, I was able to resonate with many different people and cultures all around the world. Thus far, through my journey

I learned lessons, witnessed blessings, received messages, and underwent stages of growth and triumph; one thing always in common are the powers of our mind and positivity daily no matter what we are faced with."

Today Author Daquian H. Williams is both a successful entrepreneur and community leader alike. He is a college graduate of Notre Dame College earning bachelor's degrees in Business, Political Science, and Criminal Justice. He is a loving and dedicated father who adamantly makes his daughter Serenity the focal point of his life.

Creating daily motivations and affirmations, Daquian shares his story and the secret to finding that destination of serenity through life's ups and downs that many search for. When sharing about his life, trials, and triumphs Daquian often says, "Those early mornings and late nights filled my soul with ambition and eagerness to learn more and follow my dreams. Our minds and bodies can withstand, stretch, endure, embrace and achieve so much with the right drive."

Now you are invited to take your life on a journey
to a destination of serenity

Lightning Source UK Ltd.
Milton Keynes UK
UKHW020024240522
403419UK00003B/136